50 Clean Eating Dishes

By: Kelly Johnson

Table of Contents

- Quinoa and Roasted Veggie Bowl
- Grilled Lemon Herb Chicken with Steamed Broccoli
- Avocado and Poached Egg Toast
- Baked Salmon with Garlic and Asparagus
- Sweet Potato and Black Bean Tacos
- Greek Yogurt and Berry Parfait
- Chia Seed Pudding with Almond Butter
- Turmeric Roasted Cauliflower and Chickpeas
- Spinach and Mushroom Egg Scramble
- Zucchini Noodles with Pesto and Cherry Tomatoes
- Lentil and Kale Soup
- Grilled Shrimp and Mango Salad
- Overnight Oats with Nuts and Seeds
- Roasted Brussels Sprouts with Balsamic Glaze
- Cauliflower Rice Stir-Fry
- Wild Rice and Roasted Carrot Bowl
- Grilled Portobello Mushrooms with Quinoa
- Cucumber and Avocado Gazpacho
- Almond-Crusted Baked Cod
- Stuffed Bell Peppers with Turkey and Brown Rice
- Beet and Goat Cheese Salad with Walnuts
- Roasted Butternut Squash and Quinoa Salad
- Spaghetti Squash with Marinara Sauce
- Coconut Curry Lentils
- Blueberry and Spinach Smoothie
- Baked Sweet Potato Fries with Avocado Dip
- Hummus and Veggie Wrap
- Seared Tuna with Sesame Seeds and Cabbage Slaw
- Roasted Eggplant and Tomato Salad
- Chickpea and Spinach Stew
- Fresh Tomato and Basil Bruschetta
- Homemade Granola with Nuts and Seeds
- Sautéed Kale and Garlic with Lemon
- Honey Mustard Grilled Chicken
- Spiced Carrot and Lentil Soup

- Roasted Red Pepper and Quinoa Stuffed Avocados
- Almond Butter Banana Energy Bites
- Thai-Inspired Peanut Chicken Salad
- Ginger-Turmeric Detox Tea
- Baked Falafel with Tzatziki Sauce
- Roasted Root Vegetable Medley
- Spinach and Feta Stuffed Chicken Breast
- Black Bean and Corn Salsa with Lime
- Pumpkin Seed and Apple Salad
- Grilled Veggie and Hummus Plate
- Coconut and Almond Chia Smoothie
- Garlic Roasted Chickpeas
- Oven-Baked Herb-Crusted Tofu
- Cucumber and Dill Greek Yogurt Dip
- Dark Chocolate and Nut Energy Bars

Quinoa and Roasted Veggie Bowl

Ingredients:

- ½ cup cooked quinoa
- ½ cup roasted sweet potatoes
- ½ cup roasted bell peppers
- ½ cup roasted zucchini
- 1 tablespoon olive oil
- 1 teaspoon balsamic vinegar
- Salt and pepper to taste

Instructions:

1. Toss veggies with olive oil, salt, and pepper, then roast at 400°F (200°C) for 20 minutes.
2. Place quinoa in a bowl and top with roasted vegetables.
3. Drizzle with balsamic vinegar before serving.

Grilled Lemon Herb Chicken with Steamed Broccoli

Ingredients:

- 1 boneless, skinless chicken breast
- 1 tablespoon olive oil
- 1 tablespoon lemon juice
- 1 teaspoon dried oregano
- ½ teaspoon garlic powder
- 1 cup steamed broccoli

Instructions:

1. Marinate chicken with olive oil, lemon juice, oregano, and garlic powder for 30 minutes.
2. Grill over medium heat for 6–8 minutes per side until cooked through.
3. Serve with steamed broccoli.

Avocado and Poached Egg Toast

Ingredients:

- 2 slices sourdough bread, toasted
- 1 ripe avocado, mashed
- 2 eggs
- 1 tablespoon white vinegar
- Salt, pepper, and red pepper flakes to taste

Instructions:

1. Poach eggs in simmering water with vinegar for 3–4 minutes.
2. Spread mashed avocado on toast.
3. Top with poached eggs, salt, pepper, and red pepper flakes.

Baked Salmon with Garlic and Asparagus

Ingredients:

- 1 salmon fillet
- 1 cup asparagus spears
- 1 tablespoon olive oil
- 2 cloves garlic, minced
- 1 teaspoon lemon juice
- Salt and pepper to taste

Instructions:

1. Preheat oven to 400°F (200°C).
2. Place salmon and asparagus on a baking sheet.
3. Drizzle with olive oil, garlic, lemon juice, salt, and pepper.
4. Bake for 12–15 minutes until salmon is flaky.

Sweet Potato and Black Bean Tacos

Ingredients:

- 4 small corn tortillas
- 1 cup roasted sweet potatoes, diced
- ½ cup black beans
- ¼ teaspoon cumin
- ¼ teaspoon chili powder
- 1 tablespoon lime juice
- 1 tablespoon chopped cilantro

Instructions:

1. Heat black beans with cumin, chili powder, and lime juice.
2. Fill tortillas with roasted sweet potatoes and black beans.
3. Garnish with chopped cilantro.

Greek Yogurt and Berry Parfait

Ingredients:

- 1 cup Greek yogurt
- ½ cup mixed berries
- ¼ cup granola
- 1 teaspoon honey

Instructions:

1. Layer Greek yogurt, berries, and granola in a glass.
2. Drizzle with honey before serving.

Chia Seed Pudding with Almond Butter

Ingredients:

- ¼ cup chia seeds
- 1 cup almond milk
- 1 teaspoon honey
- 1 tablespoon almond butter
- ½ teaspoon cinnamon

Instructions:

1. Mix chia seeds, almond milk, and honey.
2. Refrigerate overnight until thick.
3. Stir and top with almond butter and cinnamon.

Turmeric Roasted Cauliflower and Chickpeas

Ingredients:

- 1 cup cauliflower florets
- ½ cup canned chickpeas, drained
- 1 tablespoon olive oil
- ½ teaspoon turmeric
- ½ teaspoon cumin
- Salt and pepper to taste

Instructions:

1. Toss cauliflower and chickpeas with olive oil, turmeric, cumin, salt, and pepper.
2. Roast at 400°F (200°C) for 20–25 minutes until golden brown.

Spinach and Mushroom Egg Scramble

Ingredients:

- 2 eggs
- ½ cup spinach
- ½ cup mushrooms, sliced
- 1 tablespoon butter
- Salt and pepper to taste

Instructions:

1. Sauté mushrooms in butter for 3 minutes.
2. Add spinach and cook until wilted.
3. Scramble eggs and cook until set.
4. Season with salt and pepper.

Zucchini Noodles with Pesto and Cherry Tomatoes

Ingredients:

- 1 medium zucchini, spiralized
- ½ cup cherry tomatoes, halved
- 2 tablespoons pesto
- 1 teaspoon olive oil
- Salt and pepper to taste

Instructions:

1. Sauté zucchini noodles in olive oil for 2 minutes.
2. Add cherry tomatoes and cook for 1 more minute.
3. Toss with pesto and season with salt and pepper.

Lentil and Kale Soup

Ingredients:

- ½ cup cooked lentils
- 1 cup vegetable broth
- ½ cup chopped kale
- ½ teaspoon cumin
- ½ teaspoon garlic powder
- 1 teaspoon olive oil

Instructions:

1. Heat olive oil in a pot and sauté kale for 2 minutes.
2. Add cooked lentils, broth, cumin, and garlic powder.
3. Simmer for 10 minutes and serve warm.

Grilled Shrimp and Mango Salad

Ingredients:

- ½ lb shrimp, peeled and deveined
- 1 mango, diced
- 4 cups mixed greens
- ¼ red onion, thinly sliced
- 1 tablespoon olive oil
- 1 teaspoon lime juice
- ½ teaspoon chili powder
- ¼ cup chopped cilantro

Instructions:

1. Toss shrimp with olive oil, lime juice, and chili powder.
2. Grill shrimp over medium heat for 2–3 minutes per side.
3. Arrange mixed greens, mango, and red onion in a bowl.
4. Top with grilled shrimp and garnish with cilantro.

Overnight Oats with Nuts and Seeds

Ingredients:

- ½ cup rolled oats
- 1 cup almond milk
- 1 tablespoon chia seeds
- 1 tablespoon flaxseeds
- 1 teaspoon honey
- 2 tablespoons mixed nuts (almonds, walnuts, pecans)

Instructions:

1. Combine oats, almond milk, chia seeds, flaxseeds, and honey in a jar.
2. Refrigerate overnight.
3. Stir and top with mixed nuts before serving.

Roasted Brussels Sprouts with Balsamic Glaze

Ingredients:

- 2 cups Brussels sprouts, halved
- 1 tablespoon olive oil
- ½ teaspoon salt
- ¼ teaspoon black pepper
- 2 tablespoons balsamic glaze

Instructions:

1. Toss Brussels sprouts with olive oil, salt, and pepper.
2. Roast at 400°F (200°C) for 20–25 minutes.
3. Drizzle with balsamic glaze before serving.

Cauliflower Rice Stir-Fry

Ingredients:

- 2 cups cauliflower rice
- ½ cup bell peppers, diced
- ½ cup carrots, shredded
- 2 tablespoons soy sauce
- 1 teaspoon sesame oil
- 1 teaspoon garlic, minced
- 1 green onion, chopped

Instructions:

1. Heat sesame oil in a pan and sauté garlic for 1 minute.
2. Add bell peppers and carrots, cooking for 2–3 minutes.
3. Stir in cauliflower rice and soy sauce, cooking for another 3 minutes.
4. Garnish with green onions before serving.

Wild Rice and Roasted Carrot Bowl

Ingredients:

- ½ cup cooked wild rice
- 1 cup carrots, roasted
- 1 tablespoon olive oil
- ½ teaspoon cumin
- ½ teaspoon salt
- 1 tablespoon pumpkin seeds

Instructions:

1. Toss carrots with olive oil, cumin, and salt, then roast at 400°F (200°C) for 20 minutes.
2. Place wild rice in a bowl and top with roasted carrots and pumpkin seeds.

Grilled Portobello Mushrooms with Quinoa

Ingredients:

- 2 large Portobello mushrooms
- ½ cup cooked quinoa
- 1 tablespoon balsamic vinegar
- 1 teaspoon olive oil
- 1 teaspoon garlic powder
- ¼ cup crumbled feta cheese

Instructions:

1. Brush mushrooms with balsamic vinegar, olive oil, and garlic powder.
2. Grill over medium heat for 4–5 minutes per side.
3. Serve with quinoa and top with feta cheese.

Cucumber and Avocado Gazpacho

Ingredients:

- 1 cucumber, peeled and chopped
- 1 avocado
- 1 cup vegetable broth
- 1 teaspoon lime juice
- 1 teaspoon olive oil
- Salt and pepper to taste

Instructions:

1. Blend cucumber, avocado, vegetable broth, lime juice, olive oil, salt, and pepper until smooth.
2. Chill for at least 30 minutes before serving.

Almond-Crusted Baked Cod

Ingredients:

- 2 cod fillets
- ½ cup almonds, finely chopped
- 1 tablespoon Dijon mustard
- 1 tablespoon lemon juice
- 1 teaspoon garlic powder
- 1 teaspoon olive oil

Instructions:

1. Preheat oven to 375°F (190°C).
2. Mix almonds, garlic powder, and olive oil.
3. Spread Dijon mustard on cod fillets, then coat with almond mixture.
4. Bake for 12–15 minutes until golden brown.

Stuffed Bell Peppers with Turkey and Brown Rice

Ingredients:

- 2 bell peppers, halved and deseeded
- ½ lb ground turkey
- ½ cup cooked brown rice
- ½ cup diced tomatoes
- 1 teaspoon cumin
- 1 teaspoon chili powder
- 1 tablespoon olive oil

Instructions:

1. Heat olive oil in a pan and cook ground turkey with cumin and chili powder.
2. Stir in cooked brown rice and diced tomatoes.
3. Stuff mixture into bell peppers and bake at 375°F (190°C) for 20 minutes.

Beet and Goat Cheese Salad with Walnuts

Ingredients:

- 2 cups mixed greens
- ½ cup roasted beets, sliced
- ¼ cup crumbled goat cheese
- 2 tablespoons walnuts, chopped
- 1 tablespoon balsamic vinaigrette

Instructions:

1. Arrange mixed greens, roasted beets, goat cheese, and walnuts in a bowl.
2. Drizzle with balsamic vinaigrette before serving.

Roasted Butternut Squash and Quinoa Salad

Ingredients:

- ½ cup cooked quinoa
- 1 cup butternut squash, cubed and roasted
- 1 tablespoon olive oil
- ½ teaspoon cinnamon
- ¼ cup dried cranberries
- 2 tablespoons pumpkin seeds

Instructions:

1. Toss butternut squash with olive oil and cinnamon, then roast at 400°F (200°C) for 20 minutes.
2. Mix with cooked quinoa, dried cranberries, and pumpkin seeds before serving.

Spaghetti Squash with Marinara Sauce

Ingredients:

- 1 medium spaghetti squash
- 1 cup marinara sauce
- 1 tablespoon olive oil
- 1 teaspoon garlic powder
- ½ teaspoon salt
- ¼ cup grated Parmesan cheese (optional)
- Fresh basil for garnish

Instructions:

1. Preheat oven to 400°F (200°C).
2. Cut spaghetti squash in half and remove seeds.
3. Drizzle with olive oil, sprinkle with garlic powder and salt.
4. Bake face down for 30–40 minutes until tender.
5. Scrape flesh with a fork to create spaghetti-like strands.
6. Heat marinara sauce and pour over squash.
7. Top with Parmesan and fresh basil.

Coconut Curry Lentils

Ingredients:

- 1 cup dried lentils
- 1 cup coconut milk
- 1 cup vegetable broth
- 1 teaspoon curry powder
- ½ teaspoon turmeric
- 1 teaspoon garlic, minced
- 1 tablespoon olive oil
- ½ cup diced tomatoes

Instructions:

1. Heat olive oil in a pan and sauté garlic.
2. Add lentils, coconut milk, vegetable broth, curry powder, turmeric, and tomatoes.
3. Simmer for 25 minutes until lentils are tender.

Blueberry and Spinach Smoothie

Ingredients:

- 1 cup fresh spinach
- ½ cup frozen blueberries
- ½ banana
- 1 cup almond milk
- 1 teaspoon chia seeds

Instructions:

1. Blend all ingredients until smooth.

Baked Sweet Potato Fries with Avocado Dip

Ingredients:

- 2 sweet potatoes, cut into fries
- 1 tablespoon olive oil
- ½ teaspoon paprika
- ½ teaspoon salt
- 1 ripe avocado
- 1 tablespoon lime juice
- 1 teaspoon garlic powder

Instructions:

1. Toss sweet potato fries with olive oil, paprika, and salt.
2. Bake at 400°F (200°C) for 25 minutes, flipping halfway.
3. Mash avocado with lime juice and garlic powder for dipping.

Hummus and Veggie Wrap

Ingredients:

- 1 whole wheat tortilla
- ¼ cup hummus
- ½ cup sliced cucumbers, bell peppers, and carrots
- ¼ cup spinach or arugula

Instructions:

1. Spread hummus on tortilla.
2. Add sliced veggies and spinach.
3. Roll tightly and slice in half.

Seared Tuna with Sesame Seeds and Cabbage Slaw

Ingredients:

- 1 tuna steak
- 1 tablespoon sesame seeds
- 1 teaspoon soy sauce
- 1 teaspoon sesame oil
- 1 cup shredded cabbage
- 1 teaspoon rice vinegar

Instructions:

1. Coat tuna steak with sesame seeds and soy sauce.
2. Sear in sesame oil for 1-2 minutes per side.
3. Toss cabbage with rice vinegar and serve with tuna.

Roasted Eggplant and Tomato Salad

Ingredients:

- 1 eggplant, cubed
- 1 cup cherry tomatoes, halved
- 1 tablespoon olive oil
- 1 teaspoon balsamic vinegar
- ½ teaspoon salt

Instructions:

1. Toss eggplant and tomatoes with olive oil and salt.
2. Roast at 400°F (200°C) for 20 minutes.
3. Drizzle with balsamic vinegar before serving.

Chickpea and Spinach Stew

Ingredients:

- 1 can chickpeas, drained
- 2 cups spinach
- 1 cup vegetable broth
- 1 teaspoon cumin
- 1 teaspoon garlic, minced
- 1 tablespoon olive oil

Instructions:

1. Heat olive oil in a pot and sauté garlic.
2. Add chickpeas, spinach, vegetable broth, and cumin.
3. Simmer for 10 minutes and serve warm.

Fresh Tomato and Basil Bruschetta

Ingredients:

- 1 baguette, sliced
- 2 ripe tomatoes, diced
- 1 tablespoon olive oil
- 1 teaspoon balsamic vinegar
- 4 fresh basil leaves, chopped
- 1 garlic clove, minced

Instructions:

1. Mix tomatoes, olive oil, balsamic vinegar, basil, and garlic.
2. Toast baguette slices in the oven for 5 minutes at 375°F (190°C).
3. Spoon tomato mixture onto toasted bread.

Homemade Granola with Nuts and Seeds

Ingredients:

- 2 cups rolled oats
- ½ cup mixed nuts (almonds, walnuts, pecans)
- ¼ cup pumpkin and sunflower seeds
- ¼ cup honey or maple syrup
- 1 teaspoon cinnamon
- 1 tablespoon coconut oil

Instructions:

1. Mix all ingredients in a bowl.
2. Spread on a baking sheet and bake at 325°F (165°C) for 20 minutes, stirring halfway.

Sautéed Kale and Garlic with Lemon

Ingredients:

- 2 cups kale, chopped
- 2 cloves garlic, minced
- 1 tablespoon olive oil
- 1 teaspoon lemon juice
- Salt and pepper to taste

Instructions:

1. Heat olive oil in a pan and sauté garlic for 1 minute.
2. Add kale and cook until wilted, about 3–4 minutes.
3. Drizzle with lemon juice and season with salt and pepper.

Honey Mustard Grilled Chicken

Ingredients:

- 2 boneless, skinless chicken breasts
- 2 tablespoons honey
- 1 tablespoon Dijon mustard
- 1 tablespoon olive oil
- 1 teaspoon garlic powder
- ½ teaspoon salt
- ½ teaspoon black pepper

Instructions:

1. Whisk together honey, mustard, olive oil, garlic powder, salt, and pepper.
2. Marinate chicken in the mixture for at least 30 minutes.
3. Grill over medium heat for 6–8 minutes per side until cooked through.

Spiced Carrot and Lentil Soup

Ingredients:

- 1 cup red lentils
- 2 carrots, chopped
- 1 small onion, diced
- 2 cloves garlic, minced
- 1 teaspoon cumin
- ½ teaspoon turmeric
- 4 cups vegetable broth
- 1 tablespoon olive oil

Instructions:

1. Heat olive oil in a pot and sauté onion, garlic, and carrots for 5 minutes.
2. Add lentils, cumin, turmeric, and broth.
3. Simmer for 20–25 minutes, then blend until smooth.

Roasted Red Pepper and Quinoa Stuffed Avocados

Ingredients:

- 2 ripe avocados, halved and pitted
- ½ cup cooked quinoa
- ½ cup roasted red peppers, diced
- 1 teaspoon olive oil
- ½ teaspoon lemon juice
- Salt and pepper to taste

Instructions:

1. Mix quinoa, roasted red peppers, olive oil, lemon juice, salt, and pepper.
2. Spoon mixture into avocado halves.

Almond Butter Banana Energy Bites

Ingredients:

- 1 ripe banana, mashed
- ½ cup almond butter
- 1 cup rolled oats
- 1 tablespoon chia seeds
- 1 tablespoon honey

Instructions:

1. Mix all ingredients in a bowl.
2. Roll into small balls and refrigerate for at least 30 minutes.

Thai-Inspired Peanut Chicken Salad

Ingredients:

- 2 cups shredded cooked chicken
- ½ cup shredded carrots
- ½ cup shredded cabbage
- 2 tablespoons peanut butter
- 1 tablespoon soy sauce
- 1 teaspoon sesame oil
- 1 teaspoon lime juice
- 1 teaspoon honey
- 1 tablespoon chopped peanuts

Instructions:

1. Whisk together peanut butter, soy sauce, sesame oil, lime juice, and honey.
2. Toss with chicken, carrots, and cabbage.
3. Garnish with chopped peanuts.

Ginger-Turmeric Detox Tea

Ingredients:

- 1 teaspoon fresh ginger, grated
- ½ teaspoon turmeric powder
- 1 cup hot water
- 1 teaspoon honey
- ½ teaspoon lemon juice

Instructions:

1. Steep ginger and turmeric in hot water for 5 minutes.
2. Stir in honey and lemon juice before serving.

Baked Falafel with Tzatziki Sauce

Ingredients:

- 1 can chickpeas, drained
- 1 garlic clove, minced
- ½ teaspoon cumin
- ½ teaspoon coriander
- 2 tablespoons flour
- 1 tablespoon olive oil
- ½ teaspoon salt
- ½ cup Greek yogurt
- ¼ cup cucumber, grated
- 1 teaspoon lemon juice
- 1 teaspoon dill

Instructions:

1. Blend chickpeas, garlic, cumin, coriander, flour, olive oil, and salt.
2. Form into small patties and bake at 375°F (190°C) for 20 minutes.
3. Mix yogurt, cucumber, lemon juice, and dill for tzatziki sauce.
4. Serve falafel with tzatziki.

Roasted Root Vegetable Medley

Ingredients:

- 1 sweet potato, cubed
- 2 carrots, chopped
- 1 parsnip, chopped
- 1 tablespoon olive oil
- ½ teaspoon rosemary
- ½ teaspoon salt
- ½ teaspoon black pepper

Instructions:

1. Toss vegetables with olive oil, rosemary, salt, and pepper.
2. Roast at 400°F (200°C) for 30 minutes.

Spinach and Feta Stuffed Chicken Breast

Ingredients:

- 2 boneless, skinless chicken breasts
- 1 cup fresh spinach, chopped
- ¼ cup feta cheese, crumbled
- 1 teaspoon garlic powder
- 1 tablespoon olive oil
- Salt and pepper to taste

Instructions:

1. Slice a pocket in each chicken breast.
2. Stuff with spinach and feta.
3. Season with garlic powder, salt, and pepper.
4. Heat olive oil in a pan and sear chicken for 3 minutes per side.
5. Transfer to an oven at 375°F (190°C) and bake for 15 minutes.

Black Bean and Corn Salsa with Lime

Ingredients:

- 1 can black beans, drained
- 1 cup corn kernels
- ½ red onion, diced
- ½ red bell pepper, diced
- 1 tablespoon lime juice
- 1 tablespoon olive oil
- ¼ teaspoon cumin
- ¼ cup chopped cilantro

Instructions:

1. Mix all ingredients in a bowl.
2. Let sit for 10 minutes before serving.

Pumpkin Seed and Apple Salad

Ingredients:

- 4 cups mixed greens
- 1 apple, thinly sliced
- ¼ cup pumpkin seeds
- ¼ cup crumbled feta cheese
- 2 tablespoons dried cranberries
- 2 tablespoons balsamic vinaigrette

Instructions:

1. Toss mixed greens, apple slices, pumpkin seeds, feta, and cranberries in a bowl.
2. Drizzle with balsamic vinaigrette before serving.

Grilled Veggie and Hummus Plate

Ingredients:

- 1 zucchini, sliced
- 1 red bell pepper, sliced
- ½ eggplant, sliced
- 1 tablespoon olive oil
- ½ teaspoon garlic powder
- Salt and pepper to taste
- ½ cup hummus

Instructions:

1. Toss vegetables with olive oil, garlic powder, salt, and pepper.
2. Grill over medium heat for 3–4 minutes per side.
3. Serve with hummus on the side.

Coconut and Almond Chia Smoothie

Ingredients:

- 1 cup coconut milk
- 1 frozen banana
- 1 tablespoon almond butter
- 1 teaspoon chia seeds
- ½ teaspoon cinnamon

Instructions:

1. Blend all ingredients until smooth.
2. Pour into a glass and serve immediately.

Garlic Roasted Chickpeas

Ingredients:

- 1 can chickpeas, drained and rinsed
- 1 tablespoon olive oil
- 1 teaspoon garlic powder
- ½ teaspoon smoked paprika
- ¼ teaspoon salt

Instructions:

1. Toss chickpeas with olive oil, garlic powder, paprika, and salt.
2. Spread on a baking sheet and roast at 400°F (200°C) for 20–25 minutes.

Oven-Baked Herb-Crusted Tofu

Ingredients:

- 1 block firm tofu, pressed and sliced
- 1 tablespoon olive oil
- ½ teaspoon dried oregano
- ½ teaspoon garlic powder
- ½ teaspoon thyme
- ¼ teaspoon salt

Instructions:

1. Toss tofu slices with olive oil, oregano, garlic powder, thyme, and salt.
2. Arrange on a baking sheet and bake at 375°F (190°C) for 25 minutes, flipping halfway.

Cucumber and Dill Greek Yogurt Dip

Ingredients:

- 1 cup Greek yogurt
- ½ cucumber, grated and drained
- 1 teaspoon lemon juice
- 1 teaspoon fresh dill, chopped
- ½ teaspoon garlic powder
- Salt and pepper to taste

Instructions:

1. Mix all ingredients in a bowl.
2. Refrigerate for at least 30 minutes before serving.

Dark Chocolate and Nut Energy Bars

Ingredients:

- 1 cup rolled oats
- ½ cup mixed nuts (almonds, walnuts, cashews)
- ¼ cup dark chocolate chips
- ¼ cup honey or maple syrup
- 2 tablespoons almond butter
- 1 teaspoon vanilla extract

Instructions:

1. Mix oats, nuts, chocolate chips, honey, almond butter, and vanilla extract.
2. Press into a lined baking dish and refrigerate for at least 1 hour.
3. Cut into bars and serve.

www.ingramcontent.com/pod-product-compliance
Lightning Source LLC
LaVergne TN
LVHW061954070526
838199LV00060B/4102